When Things Go Wrong

When Things Go Wrong

A Book of Comfort

Alvin N. Rogness

Augsburg

MINNEAPOLIS

WHEN THINGS GO WRONG
A Book of Comfort
by Alvin N. Rogness

1999 Augsburg Books Edition.

Text of this edition originally appeared in *Book of Comfort,* Copyright © 1979 Augsburg Publishing House.

Cover design by Craig Claeys; interior design by Michelle L. Norstad.

Acknowledgments
Scripture quotations are from the New Revised Standard Version © 1989 by the Division of Christian Education of the National Council of the Churches of Christ in the United States of America. Used by permission.

Library of Congress Cataloging-in-Publication Data
Rogness, Alvin N., 1906-
    When things go wrong : a book of comfort / by Alvin N. Rogness. —
Augsburg Books ed.
    p. cm.
    Includes bibliographical references.
    ISBN 0-8066-3841-9 (alk. paper)
    1. Consolation. 2. Failure (Christian theology) 3. Christian life—
Lutheran authors. I. Title.
BV4905.2.R633 1999
248.8'6—dc21   98-48282
                                       CIP

Manufactured in the U.S.A.   AF 9-3841

03   02   01   00   99   1   2   3   4   5   6   7   8   9   10

Contents

Preface

You and I are on a road of sharp turns and sudden dips. And there's fog, thick fog. Sometimes boulders block the way. We neglect the map and are lured into detours. Weary, we may want to give up. We cry for comfort.

There is comfort. Years ago God said,

> Comfort, comfort my people. . . .
> Speak tenderly to Jerusalem, and proclaim to her
> that her hard service has been completed,
> that her sin has been paid for,
> that she has received from the Lord's hand
> double for all her sins.

God yearns to comfort us—but on God's terms and in God's way. If I call on God, I understand that he may have to stop me in my tracks and turn me around before he can be gentle. God may have to use the scalpel before he can heal my pain.

In these short chapters I've tried to describe stretches along the road. I've traveled many of them. I'm old enough to have learned a little about them. But I'm no heroic traveler. Many times I've rejected God's comfort and tried to go it alone. Often I've been puzzled about the kind of comfort God seemed to give.

I have the map, the Word of God, God's wisdom and promises. And I have a Friend who has walked the way before me and who walks with me now. His hand is on me to lead me and to hold me. There is no greater comfort than that.

1

When You Think You're a Failure

By God's standards we are all failures. There's none really good, says the psalmist. By God's incredibly high measurements of love and holiness, none of us will pass.

By the world's standards, we may be successes or failures, but it may make little difference to God how we rate. God accepts us as sons and daughters and sweeps us into his kingdom of love, no matter how well or ill we score. We belong to him and can afford to fail.

But we will be troubled by worldly standards, many of them trivial, some of them fraudulent. Money, for instance. What was his top salary? How much of an estate did he leave? It was said of Abraham Lincoln, who died poor, "He forgot to collect his earnings."

In our rapidly changing society, some people lose their

jobs at fifty and have to start over again. It's a crushing experience. Why hadn't he climbed high enough on the ladder to ensure his place until retirement? Unless he can remember that he was caught in the storm of economic forces over which he had little or no control (like a tornado wrecking the house he had just built), he's likely to think himself a failure.

We may set goals that almost guarantee failure. A runner who trains to run the 100-yard dash in 9.5, and does it in 9.8, has failed—because he set his goals too high. Had he set out to run the distance in 11 seconds, he would have been a great success by the goals he had set. There's nothing wrong, is there, in setting ideals too high, and reaching out for them, and failing? Jesus told us to love our neighbors as ourselves, knowing full well that we would never be able to kill our self-concerns to that degree, but that in trying we might come a long way toward the goal. We are to dream the impossible dream!

What fathers and mothers, having seen the high hopes they've had for their children shattered, haven't asked themselves where they failed? They may have failed (or maybe not), but they must remember that a child is not a piece of clay that necessarily yields to the loving and wise hand of a parent. Children are independent beings who insist on finding their own way. No one, not even a parent, can be held responsible for the failure of another.

Failure may sometimes be the closing of one door and the opening of another. In my twenty years as a seminary president, I have known several students who failed in the highly competitive examinations for medical school and who turned to theology. Becoming excellent pastors, they later were convinced that they were finding greater satisfaction than they would have found in medicine.

Thousands of people can look back on failures that turned them toward opportunities of unpredictable success. It could well be that the most unfortunate are those who have never known failure. If everything has gone their way, they may become proud, condescending, and insensitive to the hurts and anxieties of others.

It is comforting to know that we have a God who wants us to set such high goals for ourselves that we must fail. Even more comforting it is that whatever our failures, whether by his standards or by the standards of the world, God loves us still, and honors us as sons and daughters in his kingdom.

Be strong and take heart, all you who hope in the Lord.
Psalm 31:24

2

When You Can't Forgive Yourself

God can forgive you. Other people can forgive you. Do you ever have the right to forgive yourself?

If you mean to find excuses for yourself, no, you don't have that right. The shame is yours to bear. Try as you will, you can't erase something wretched in the past and pretend that it never happened. You are a responsible human being, and you can't pass the buck to God or to others.

That doesn't mean that you have to be weighed down or crushed by the past. You place the past in God's hands, and God forgives. But neither God's forgiveness nor the forgiveness of others will alter the past. You'll have to live with its sadness. To pretend that it never happened is to escape into fantasy, and there's no healing in that.

Once forgiven by God (and by others, if possible), you

have a duty to let the past be the past. You neither honor God nor help yourself by pulling the past into the present and rehearsing what can't be changed. God says, "I will remember your sins no more." God forgets them, wipes them away as if they had never happened. What God can do, you cannot do. You cannot blot out your memories. They'll be like a cloud of hovering melancholy, but they need not be a load on your back. God tells you to "throw off everything that hinders . . . and run the race."

A pastor heard the anguished confession of a woman who had been unfaithful to her husband. He gave her the absolution, God's assurance of forgiveness in Christ. Upon leaving, she asked, "Shall I tell my husband?" He answered, "What is there to tell? It's all gone." He was saying that God had forgiven and forgotten, and the sin was obliterated. No need to tell. She too had a duty to forget. And you do too.

There is no way to be rid of the burden of remorse but to give it all to God. Even King David, who had committed adultery with Bathsheba and had murdered her husband Uriah, discovered that he couldn't brush it aside.

When I kept silent, my body wasted away through
my groaning all day long.
For day and night your hand was heavy upon me. . . .
Then I acknowledged my sin to you. . . .
and you forgave the guilt of my sin.

The memory no doubt was with him until he died. But he went on, with God's forgiveness and blessing, to be Israel's greatest king.

If God couldn't use people with sad memories, or bless them, there'd be no one to use. Peter denied Christ, and other disciples abandoned him in the crisis. St. Augustine wasted years in debauched youth.

To remember the sins of the past, sad as they may be, is also to be on the alert to avoid them in the future. They act as radar, setting off the danger signal as new temptations loom.

We may try other ways than God's way, but they won't work. It won't do to say "everybody does it, so I'm no worse than others." You can't commit adultery and get any genuine comfort in knowing others who do. You can't cheat on a contract or on your income tax and find consolation in knowing others cheat too. Nor can you lose your temper and speak cruel words to someone you love and brush it aside with, "Well, that's the way I am." You have generated memories that will clamor for some place to rest. They will roam your soul like ghosts until you put them in the only place that can divest them of their power—before the cross of Christ.

Don't talk about forgiving yourself. Let God do the forgiving. Then go on to face the present and the future in the promises of God's comfort and blessing.

> *"For I will forgive their wickedness and will remember their sins no more."*
>   *Hebrews 8:12*

3

When You Come in Second

It isn't true that everyone loves a winner. Let us admit that it's not easy to love those who came in first in the race for wealth and power and prestige. If you come in second you drop back with the rest of us, the losers. We understand you and like you, because you didn't win. In our own way, we'll try to comfort you.

Let's take a look at the people who always need to be at the top. If they're students who set out to be at the head of the class, they may fall into some very unappealing ways. They may be secretly delighted when others fail, distressed when others succeed. They may lose their capacity to rejoice with those who rejoice, weep with those who weep. They certainly are not disposed to help someone get on. They may become quietly proud and priggish about their own excellence. They may even become unfair and take unjust advantage of others who are competing.

How about those who strive for excellence but do not need to be first? They use well the gifts God has given them. They are competitive and enjoy others who are better than they are. They study hard, play hard, and enjoy people. If, at graduation, someone has outdistanced them and is valedictorian, they are genuinely glad to congratulate him or her, because they did not need to win.

It may not be quite as simple if you are a contractor and are bidding a job. To come in second is to lose the job altogether. Haven't you known builders who simply move on with "you win some and you lose some," and turn to the next bidding? They have no rancor or bitterness toward the winner.

I've known people running for office who are like that. They give the race all they've got, never stooping to deceit or subterfuge. If they lose, they accept this as part of the process and go on to alternatives of service.

I suspect that people who can take their losses with grace have learned some of God's great lessons. They probably recognize that, with their limited wisdom, they cannot always know what is good for them. They know, too, that God has more than one door to fullness of life and that when one door closes other may be opening.

Victor Hugo tells of sitting in his study one summer day when a bee flew in through the open window and began trying to find its way out again. It flew about frantically, dashing its little body against one pane and another. Victor Hugo picked up a towel and tried to direct it back to the open window. Mistaking his benevolent motives, the bee beat its body against the towel and soared about from one end of the room to the other. At long last, Mr. Hugo got it near the open window, and suddenly smelling the flowers, the bee darted out to freedom.

To lose the top spot or a contract or an election may in some mysterious way be destiny edging us to an open window. Who knows? The great comfort is knowing that the purpose of life is to be a servant, loving and helping others. This is the one clue Jesus gave for greatness, for winners, if you will.

Living two doors from our home was a man who, in his bid for a second term as governor of Minnesota, came in second by a hair. Far from retreating in bitterness, Elmer L. Andersen discovered many other doors of service to the church and community. He became chairman of the University of Minnesota board of regents, chairman of a great foundation, and finally a newspaper publisher. Another "neighbor," Hubert H. Humphrey, missed the presidency by scant margin, then returned to the Senate to spend his years as a troubadour battling for causes dear to him, and against the cancer that at last brought him to bay. He received the country's love and such accolades as are given to few presidents. Anderson and Humphrey, both coming in second, did not need the winner's door to reach the road to great service.

When some door closes, God probably won't spend his time stroking your hand and weeping with you. God has better ways to comfort you, turning you away from your defeat to look ahead, tantalizing you with hope and with opportunities for something better.

Best of all, God reassures you that you are his child, and that if your path should be strewn with what seem to be defeats and failures, God will never let you down, but will be with you all the way until a final door opens and you step out of death into the winnings he has in store for you.

> *Serve wholeheartedly, as if you were serving the Lord, not men, because you know that the Lord will reward everyone for whatever good he does.*
>   *Ephesians 6:7–8*

4

When Your Marriage Is in Trouble

Marriage rests on two foundations: love and a promise. You came to love each other. Then you appeared before God and society and promised "to love her, comfort her, honor and keep her in sickness and in health, and, forsaking all others, keep only to her, so long as we both shall live." Each made the same promise to the other. Implied in that promise was another promise—that if God gave you children, together you would love them and care for them as long as you lived.

The feeling of love alone is never strong enough to keep your marriage going. Feelings are up and down—but duty is constant. You made a promise. In days when love is strained and seems to fade, duty takes over. Love itself has a chance to grow strong and mellow only when it is reinforced by promise and duty.

Every marriage runs into some rocky stretches. To give up and get off the road doesn't mean you'll end up on a smooth stretch. More than likely, you'll veer off into a jungle of pretense, remorse, and shame. Your companions from then on are the ghosts of what might have been.

It's possible to explain, perhaps even to justify, the increase of divorce rates today. But whatever the circumstances, you can't justify breaking a promise. You can't find excuses for robbing your children of love and security. Any defense you make for your right to pleasure or fulfillment will be phony. Neither God nor any code of honor will accept your defense.

These broad statements may seem harsh. A soldier may think it harsh to be told that if need be he may have to die for his country. It's equally true for a father and mother—if need be they'll have to put their own fulfillment aside for the good of the family. They may not recognize it, but such commitment is the key to fulfillment for them.

Marriage always brings together two imperfect people. Each has good qualities and each has not-so-good qualities. The romantic notion that, with marriage, faults disappear is nonsense. To be sure, each may help the other overcome undesirable traits, but that takes some doing. Unless they are vigilant, they may actually intensify bad qualities in each other.

If both partners defend their right to personal fulfillment (whatever fulfillment may mean), they should never have married. Service—not fulfillment—is the name of the marriage game. Fulfillment is the fairy that steals in as you go about loving and helping each other. It will elude you if you seek it. Aim at loving and serving and you'll get fulfillment thrown in. That's the way God designed life, and you can't cheat the architect.

Nothing frightens me as much as today's increase in divorce, because it sets children adrift on a stormy sea. No matter if both separated parents assure the children of their love, the children will be haunted: "They didn't love me enough to swallow their selfishness and spare me this great pain." And the pain won't be less because there are more children today with the same pain. If the boat capsizes and you're drowning, there's no joy in knowing that others are drowning too. What ghastly price will our society pay in the future? Children in today's world are insecure enough without having their parents remove the most important prop of all.

It matters little how successful a man is in business or profession if he defaults on his highest assignment as husband and father. And it's a sorry bargain for a wife and mother to succeed as a writer or artist if on the way she has scuttled her family.

I know there is forgiveness with God for all failures. I do not forget that marvelous truth. But not even God can remove all the wreckage. "The bird with the broken pinion never flew as high again."

Whenever you think the road is rocky (and it would be strange if you never ran into such a stretch), remember that if you decide to get off the road, you'll probably find any other road worse—not only rocky, but with no road map at all.

The real comfort lies in keeping the promise, even when it means enduring temporary distress. People who have done just that can tell you there are good stretches ahead. Love itself revives and grows mellower with understanding. And your children and grandchildren will grow strong in your love.

23

Submit to one another out of reverence for Christ.
Ephesians 5:21

5

When Your Children Rebel

When young people hurt, they rebel, or at least seem to rebel. We, their parents and elders, have a hard time understanding why. Why, when we provide them with everything they need? We give them food and shelter, schooling, time for pleasure. What else do they want, or need?

Rebellion in youth is nothing new. Every generation has to find its way to selfhood and independence. Their creator gave them that right. On the way they have to defy us. They dare not have their will swallowed up by ours. They would become zombies, puppets.

But has there ever been such defiance as today? Has any generation of youth so lashed out against the normal restrictions and standards of society?

Before giving an easy yes to that question, I go back to

my own youth in a small South Dakota village. We had the shelter of good homes, but we dug a cave in a hillside for our private club, out of bounds to our elders. We rolled crushed cigar stubs into newspapers and smoked clandestine cigarettes. We sneaked off to barn dances. On Halloween night we drove the town constable to distraction by tipping over every privy in the village. We paired off as couples, crowded into some father's Ford, and did our petty petting on dark country roads. I remember vividly the night my father met me at the door (about 10 p.m., I suppose) and asked, "Do you think your home is just a place to eat and sleep?" I was furious to think that he did not trust me to make my own decisions.

That was more than fifty years ago. Our rebellions were within a well-ordered and supportive world, with parents, grandparents, uncles, and aunts hovering around. We grew up with the strength of the tribe. If anyone were to attack me, he'd have to take on all my uncles and aunts. Families were secure; if any man had divorced his wife in our town he would have had to leave. I had bleachers all around me, filled not only with family but with all the grown-ups in the township, cheering me on when I did well and groaning when I failed.

All sorts of young people today run the race with only silence from the bleachers. It's a lonely race. Grandparents are a thousand miles away, uncles and aunts scattered to both coasts and overseas, parents often busy with double jobs, harried by their own affluence, or casualties of the divorce courts.

Nor was it the village alone that seemed safe in my youth. The world itself seemed secure. When my son, at the age of fourteen, asked me what chance he and his friends had of living out a normal lifetime, I was stunned into silence. I would never have asked that at the age of fourteen. But that was before the bomb, before the clamorous voices predicting catastrophes of overpopulation, world hunger, and exhaustion of energy. I suddenly realized that his was a different world. His hurt was far deeper than the normal frustrations of growing up.

Is it any wonder that with their hurts they run, and don't know where to run? In a world growing increasingly unsafe, where can they find refuge? The police courts, the half-way houses, and the gangs are hardly the bleachers they need.

If there ever was a time when society needed parents who, for the sake of their children, would forget about their own self-fulfillment and look to the higher claims of their children's right to love and safety, it is now. Now, when the world of uncles and aunts and grandparents is largely gone. If God is to reach children with the comfort they so desperately need, parents will have to be his agents. All our YMCAs and YWCAs, all our schools, all our community clubs, even our churches cannot possibly fill the bleachers reserved for parents.

When young people cry "The future is now," and plunge into a bewildering maze of experience, let us listen. Isn't this the cry of someone who would like to dream of a promising tomorrow, who would like to find a solid road of abiding values, who more than anything else wants to find something worth giving a lifetime to?

And the tragedy is that they so seldom find this in us, their elders. If they have been brought up in the church and stirred by the magnetic figure of Jesus, with his call for followers who will serve their world, they often are disillusioned by the pursuit of wealth and prestige and comfort and pleasure they see in their parents and in others who sit smug and indifferent in the pews. It is we, their elders, who rob them of the dream, the tried road, the treasure worth giving up everything to have. If we listen well, it may not be the voice of rebellion we hear, but the voice of the judge indicting and sentencing us.

I cannot escape the conviction that the church is the only place where the lonely and tortured children of this uneasy age can find their bearings. Here, again and again, over and over, they are given the good news of a God who cares. Even a father and mother may forget their child, says the psalmist, but not this great and good God. I remember the story of the poor, orphaned boy who was taunted for his faith in God by someone saying, "It seems God has forgotten you," and his replying, "God hasn't forgotten, but the people God sent to care for me have forgotten." Increasingly congregations are realizing that they have been sent to listen, to try to understand, to dispel loneliness, to heal wounds, and to reach out the hand of kindness instead of raising the voice of judgment.

But it takes unusual insight, patience, and love to understand. When to escape their loneliness, they form tight gangs, when they seek refuge in careless sex, when in desperation they take to drugs, can we understand that they are in panic to find the dream? Or that, when apprehended for shoplifting, they are imitating their elders' mad appetite for things?

It may seem more responsible for us to come down hard on their defections, and to use the harsh instruments of authority, law and order, to quell their rebellion. Are we not God's agents for discipline? Indeed we are. And if we discipline in love, they will understand. But without love, our efforts will but breed more rebellion.

We can take our clue from him who loved to the uttermost, to a cross.

> I did not come to judge the world but to save it.

> Do not judge, or you too will be judged. . . . First take the plank out of your own eye, and then you will see clearly to remove the speck from your brother's eye.

Jane Addams, the founder of Chicago's famous Hull House, tells of an instance in her childhood that shaped her life. She had lied to her father, a stern Dutch Calvinist, and after days of tortured conscience, she came to him with her confession of wrong. He picked her up in his arms and said, "Jane, remember that whatever you do, I will always love you." The contagion of this love, a love like that of God, drove Jane to found the great refuge for people whose

29

lives were in shambles.

There is no healing for loneliness, fear, and failure to equal this kind of love. Since Jesus brought it into a troubled world almost 2000 years ago, it has given hope and meaning to hundreds of millions of lives. It still brings that hope!

> *Father, do not exasperate your children; instead bring them up in the training and instruction of the Lord.*
> *Ephesians 6:4*

6

When Grace Seems Too Easy

You tell me that the Christian faith doesn't appeal to you because it's too easy. Your preacher talks about God being so gracious that he lets you off. What's happened to his demands, or doesn't he really have any? If he has some, doesn't he enforce them? Even the Rotary Club makes you attend meetings. If you miss, you have to make it up.

You say you feel that you're not taken seriously. What kind of God doesn't seem to care what you do, as long as you depend on him to see you through? This whole matter of grace, and grace alone, has you baffled. It seems too easy to be true.

You raise some disturbing questions. The apostle Paul admitted that this whole matter of God's grace would seem an offense, a stumbling block, sheer foolishness.

I'm reminded of what John Steinbeck observed in his delightful book, *Travels with Charlie.* He had drifted into a little country church in Vermont on a Sunday morning. Here are his reactions:

> The service did my heart and I hope my soul some good. It is our practise now, at least in the large cities, to find from our psychiatric priesthood that our sins aren't really sins at all but accidents that are set in motion by forces beyond our control. There was no such nonsense in this church. . . . For some years now God has been a pal to us, practising togetherness, and that causes the same emptiness a father does playing softball with his son. But this Vermont God cared enough about me to go to a lot of trouble kicking the hell out of me. He put my sins in a new perspective. Whereas they had been small and mean and nasty and best forgotten, this minister gave them some size and bloom and dignity. I hadn't been thinking very well of myself for some years, but if my sins had this dimension there was some pride left. I wasn't a naughty child but a first rate sinner, and I was going to catch it. . . . I felt so revived in spirit that I put five dollars in the plate.

Far from minimizing the importance of our sins (or making light of God's laws), the Christian message that, through God's mercy, a person is justified or made right, takes our wrongdoing with terrifying seriousness. Your best performance won't set things right. It took the life and death and resurrection of God the Son, Jesus Christ, to meet the demands of the exalted requirements that God makes for you and me.

It could be that God's way of grace seems to bland, too soothing, too easy—because we have not seriously tried meeting the demands of God's law. Have you tried to love the Lord with all your heart, and your neighbor as yourself? Have you tried to do to others what you would they should do to you? And how about righteousness, purity of heart, the forgiving spirit—have you been striving for these goals?

Paul did, and Luther did—with an intensity that finally drove them to the wall. The demands of God became a towering mountain impossible to scale. They had no alternative but to give up. If they were to live with God, or even decently with themselves, they had to find another way. They had to throw themselves on the sheer mercy of God.

Most of us have never given God's demands this kind of try. We've tended to tailor his demands to our capacities or to society's expectations, so we've escaped both the fury of his law and the glory of his grace.

Our difficulties with grace may mean that we come to the second chapter of the book before reading the first. In the first chapter a man tries every which way to keep his business afloat, but he fails utterly and collapses into bankruptcy. It's in the second chapter that his friend comes along, pays his bills, and gives him a new capital to start afresh.

Because we don't take seriously God's fierce demands for holiness and mercy and love and purity and honesty and selflessness, we fail to understand that we are bankrupt before God. And if you think you have reasonably good credit, what's so great about your friend investing money in you? What's so wonderful about God's grace, if you believe you have the investments of a fairly decent life to fall back on?

We face two courts. The first is the society in which we live. It's fairly easy to get a good verdict here (and a nice obituary) simply by being a decent citizen. The second court is the supreme court, the high tribunal of God, where even the secret motives of the heart come under sentence. The psalmist cried, "If you, O Lord, kept a record of sins,

O Lord, who could stand?" Here not only the evil we have done comes under survey, but in addition the massive amount of good we might have done but neglected. In this court you won't ask for justice. You'll have but one cry, "God be merciful to me."

Here grace enters the picture. The God who sits on the bench is the same God who died on a cross to rescue us from the court's condemnation.

You may well ask, "If I have never stood terrified before God's high court, can I find any comfort at the foot of the cross? If the court is not real for me, will grace ever seem real?"

And still another question, "If I find myself at the foot of the cross, am I never again to be troubled by the court?"

Yes and no. Until you die, you are two people. You are the old Adam, bad and selfish, but you are also new in Christ. You shift from one self to the other. The bad you ought to stand terrified before the court. The new you should revel in the freedom and forgiveness of the cross.

If the terror of the court fades away and you forget all about it, the wonder of the cross may fade too. Your life is like a teeter-totter; the lower one end is down, the higher the other. The more bankrupt your own efforts to obey

God's high law, the greater the glory of his having done it for you. If you've taken God out of the courtroom, you'll probably not find him at the cross either.

Nor is the new you done with God's demands. They exist no longer as a brief in the courtroom, but they're still there—as a guide along the road with God. The new you seeks ways to thank God for grace by doing precisely those things that earlier tormented you as law.

When you complain that grace seems too soothing and bland, you're really complaining that our whole society, including the church, has taken the courtroom too casually. We have allowed the high bench to be empty—no judge in sight. And if we're not even important enough to be judged, we're in deep trouble. Steinbeck was right. In the courtroom we feel important again.

If you're important enough to send to hell, you're important enough to be rescued for heaven. This is what grace is all about.

> *For it is by grace you have been saved, through faith—and this not from yourselves, it is the gift of God—not by works, so that no one can boast.*
> *Ephesians 2:8–9*

7

When You Can't Laugh at Yourself

We all wear masks. We try to be—or pretend to be—
something other than we are. In one sense, we are clowns.

There's nothing basically wrong with trying or pre-
tending. Among other things, it's necessary if we are to
grow. A child pretends to manage a spoon and spills her
food; later she sits down to play her first piece on the
piano and strikes the wrong keys. "Don't laugh at her—
she's trying," her mother warns.

Laughter, like words, is language. It can be cruel or
kind. The moment people laugh, they let you into the
secrets of their character. If they laugh at your discomfort
or your pain, they tell you that they disdain you, or at
least that they're insensitive. If, on the other hand, they
laugh at their own foibles or embarrassments, even at their

limitations and failures, they tell you that they have wisdom and strength and charity. You love them for it.

God must want us to laugh. Only to humans, of all his creatures, did he give the gift of laughter. Not to dogs, not to horses, nor to hyenas. If we can't laugh, we have lost some of our humanness.

To laugh when it's right to laugh and to weep when it's right to weep is to be wise and good. To laugh when you ought to weep or to weep when you ought to laugh is to be a cad or a fool. You wouldn't want to go fishing with someone whose character is that twisted.

People who can laugh at themselves do take themselves seriously, but not too seriously. They understand that there will always be a gap between what they ought to be and what they are, between what they ought to do and what they do. This is essentially a profound religious insight. It is the biblical truth that we are fallen creatures. The human will and mind and emotions have all been damaged by the presence of evil. We are doomed to fall short of perfection, try as we will.

We can find release from the destructive force of this tragic gap by being captured by the great biblical truth that Christ has bridged the gap for us: "Though your sins are like scarlet, they shall be as white as snow." In his mercy God has wiped away the gap, so we can stand before God as if we were perfect.

But only before God. Until we die, we will struggle with the gap that yawns between what we ought to do and what we do. We will yield to temptations, losing our tempers, neglecting our neighbors, becoming defensive, yielding to self-pity, blaming others.

We can deal with this gap in two ways. We can grieve over it, and we should. And we can chuckle over it. We can laugh at ourselves. This is the sense of humor the Lord wants us to have. Laughter is the release valve to the tragic. Tragedy and comedy are two sides of the same coin.

In some areas of life it's more difficult to manage a sense of humor. The Christian faith is one. Over and over again, throughout history, people have pretended to have the one truth and have been totally without humor in dealing with others who lay claim to having the truth. Christians have been separated from one another, churches have been riven, wars have been fought—all because people lost sight of the gap between what a person may know and not know. Few theologians have been able to laugh at themselves as they attempt to define religious truth.

Karl Barth, an eminent twentieth-century theologian, may be an exception. He is able to chuckle over his efforts:

> The angels laugh at old Karl. They laugh at him because he tries to grasp the truth of God in a book of dogmatics. They laugh at the fact that volume follows volume and each is thicker than the previous one. As they laugh, they say to one another, "Look! Here he comes now with his little pushcart full of volumes of dogmatics." And they laugh about the men who write so much about Karl Barth instead of writing about the things he is trying to write about. Truly the angels laugh.

Politics is another area in which humor is sparse. Few people are able to take a serious position in the political arena and, in arguing or discussing issues, back away from their seriousness to chuckle over their doctrinaire opinions.

Humor is difficult, too, for those who experience loss of security. To lose one's farm or one's investments—this is serious business. Not many people are able to say with Job, "Naked I came from my mother's womb, and naked I will depart." To relax and say, "The money was never really mine in the first place," and to go on without being crushed, is to have a wisdom that only a religious sense of humor can provide.

Life is full of situations less critical than one's religion or one's security. You have weaknesses and foibles; others have them too. You should be able to laugh at your own, and look with charity at the ones others have. I like these lines from Kipling's *If*:

> If you can keep your head when all about
> Are losing theirs and blaming it on you;
> If you can trust yourself when all men doubt you,
> But make allowance for their doubting too;
> If you can wait and not be tired by waiting,
> Or being lied about, don't deal in lies,
> Or being hated, don't give way to hating,
> And yet don't look too good, nor talk too wise;
> Yours is the earth.

Archbishop Fischer, late of Canterbury, had the light touch a sense of humor bestows. Upon his retirement, he said that most of his life he had been able to get up in the morning with anticipation to discover what bad news the morning mail might bring, but that now, having lost a little zest for it, he thought he ought to retire. He was able to laugh at himself and to deal in a spirit of humor with the limitations of others.

In his fascinating book, Scaramouche, Sabatini describes his gallant Frenchman: "He was born with the gift of laughter, and a sense that the world was mad." Sabatini's young nobleman moves through a world of intrigue with unparalleled courage, integrity, and charity, but always as if quietly laughing at himself and at the world around him. With a saving sense of humor, he is never a cynic.

It may be that genuine, healing laughter can come only with an honest appraisal of the human beings God has created—made in the image of God, yet fallen creatures, the victims of their own wretchedness and foolhardiness. In the gap between these poles is the tragedy and comedy of the human life. Deep down, we know we belong at the heights with God, and in our own blundering, rebellious, and blind way we're trying to climb back up. We weep for—and laugh at—ourselves.

The only way we can laugh with charity, both at ourselves and at our world, is to remember that the God who gave us life and who has redeemed it understands us, and that he lets us use this priceless gift of laughter to give the journey back to him a touch of merriment.

> *A cheerful heart is good medicine.*
> *Proverbs 17:22*

For Further Reading

Living Between Jobs: Meditations When You're Looking for Work
Harriet E. Crosby

From Stalemate to Soulmate: A Guide to Mature, Committed,
Loving Relationships
Michael Obsatz, Ph.D.

Jesus, Remember Me: Words of Assurance from Martin Luther
edited by Barbara Owen

Welcoming Change: Discovering Hope in Life's Transitions
James E. Miller

Wrestling with Depression: A Spiritual Guide to Reclaiming Life
William and Lucy Hulme

Nine Challenges for Parents: Leading Your Child into
Responsible Adulthood
Lucy and William Hulme

Liferails: Holding Fast to God's Promises
Scott Walker

Our Hope for Years to Come: The Search for Spiritual Sanctuary
Reflections and Photographs
Martin Marty and Micah Marty